Infinity Prime Donna Casey

"This fractal is a classic spiral, which is my favorite, and I'm always amazed at the variations and the endlessly repeating patterns that can be created out of such a primary shape." – **Donna Casey**

Investigations

IN NUMBER, DATA, AND SPACE®

Photographs

Every effort has been made to secure permission and provide appropriate credit for photographic material. The publisher deeply regrets any omission and pledges to correct errors called to its attention in subsequent editions.

Unless otherwise acknowledged, all photographs are the property of Scott Foresman, a division of Pearson Education.

Photo locators denoted as follows: Top (T), Center (C), Bottom (B), Left (L), Right (R), Background (Bkgd).

69 ™Courtesy of Campbell Soup Company

Editorial offices: Glenview, Illinois • Parsippany, New Jersey • New York, New York
Sales offices: Boston, Massachusetts • Duluth, Georgia
Glenview, Illinois • Coppell, Texas • Sacramento, California • Mesa, Arizona

The Investigations curriculum was developed by TERC, Cambridge, MA.

This material is based on work supported by the National Science Foundation ("NSF") under Grant No.ESI-0095450. Any opinions, findings, and conclusions or recommendations expressed in this material are those of the author(s) and do not necessarily reflect the views of the National Science Foundation.

ISBN: 0-328-24023-0

ISBN: 978-0-328-24023-4

UNIT 1 Who Is in School Today?

UNIT 2 Counting and Comparing

UNIT 3 What Comes Next?

UNIT 4 Measuring and Counting

UNIT 5 Make a Shape, Build a Block

UNIT 6 How Many Do You Have?

UNIT 7 Sorting and Surveys

How Many Apples?

Count how many apples Meg picked.

Meg's Apples:

How many apples did Meg pick? _____

Sorting Shapes

NOTE Students sort shapes based on a particular attribute.

Circle ⭕ the shapes that are gray .

Put an ✕ through the shapes that have stripes .

   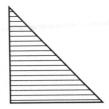   

      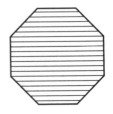

      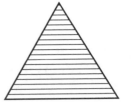

How Many Ladybugs?

Count how many ladybugs Jack found.

NOTE Students practice counting and writing numbers.

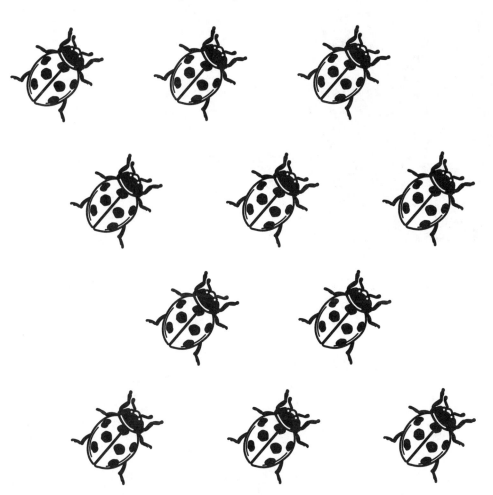

How many ladybugs did Jack find? _____

Counting My Family

Here is Emma's family.

NOTE Students count the members of their family.

Draw yourself and your family.

How many people are in your family? _____

Grab and Count

Grab a handful. Show what you grabbed.
Show how many.

Grab a handful. Show what you grabbed.
Show how many.

Roll and Record Recording Sheet

						6
						5
						4
						3
						2
						1

Ten-Frame

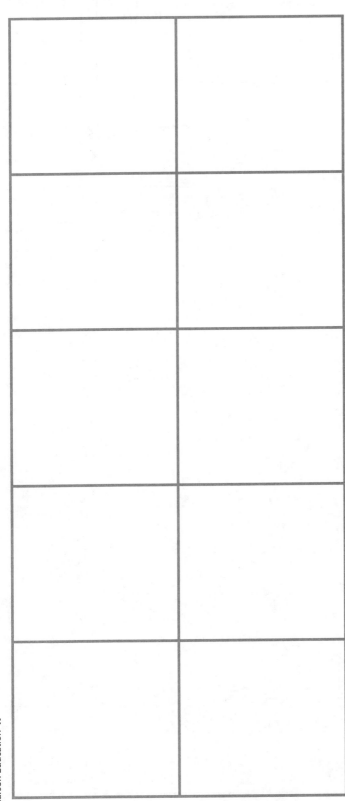

My Inventory Bag

Show what was in your bag.
Show how many.

How Many Are There?

Jeff went shopping.

Draw how many things he got.

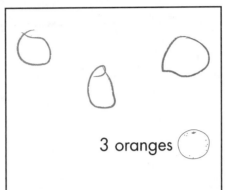

3 oranges

NOTE Students draw pictures to represent a given amount.

4 balls

7 apples

12 carrots

9 books

Counting and Comparing

Longer or Shorter?

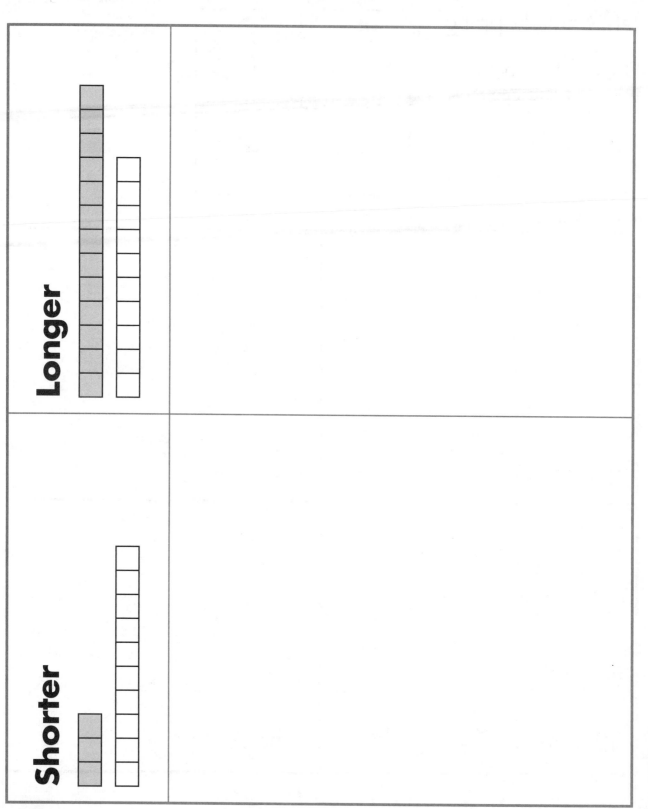

Which Is Longer?

Circle the picture
that is longer.

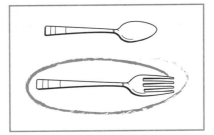

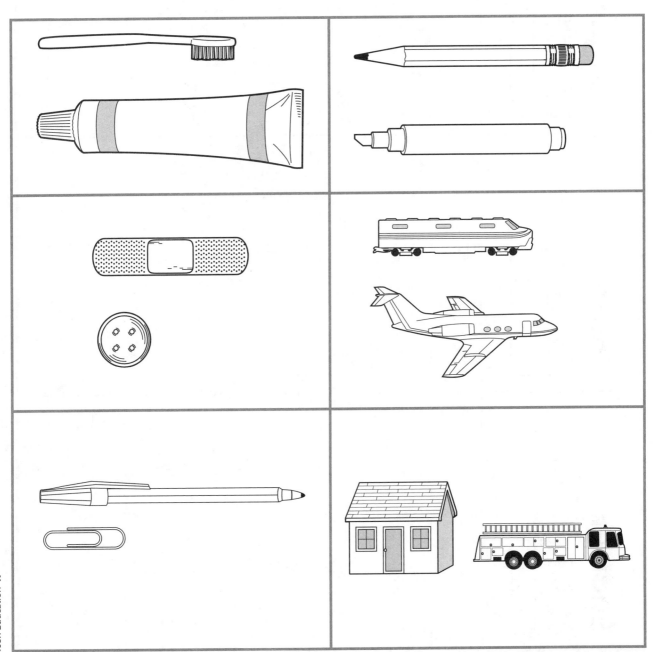

Comparing Names

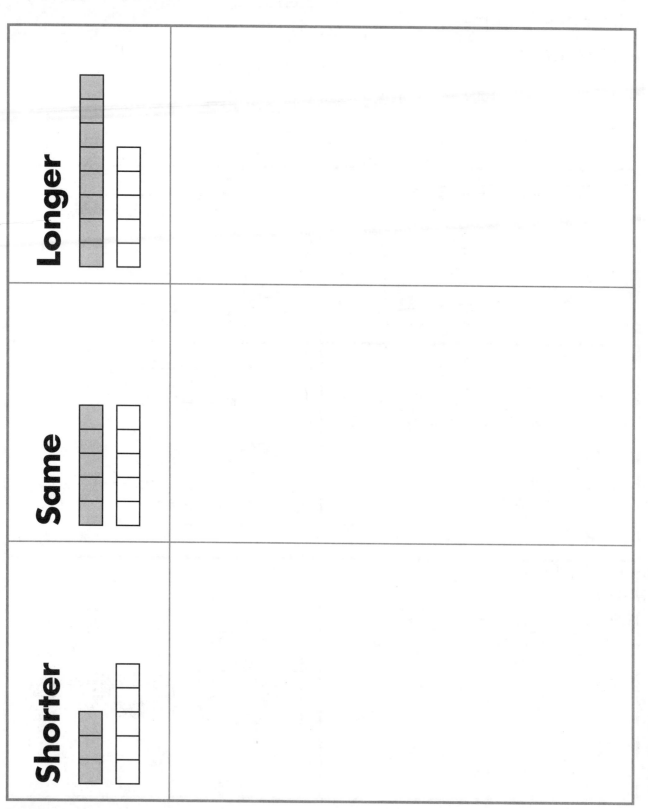

Names at Home

Write the names of people at home. Circle the name with the most letters.

> **NOTE** In class, students counted the number of letters in their names and compared names to find out which are longer and shorter. Tonight, students count and compare the number of letters in the names of the people at home and determine which is the longest.

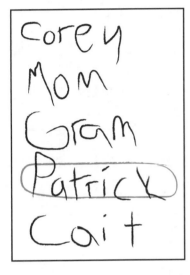

Corey
Mom
Gram
(Patrick)
Cait

Ordering Names

Pick 4 name towers. Put them in order.
Record your work.

Pick 4 name towers. Put them in order.
Record your work.

Name _____   Date _____

Counting and Comparing

Ordering Cards

Pick 4 cards. Put them in order.
Record your work.

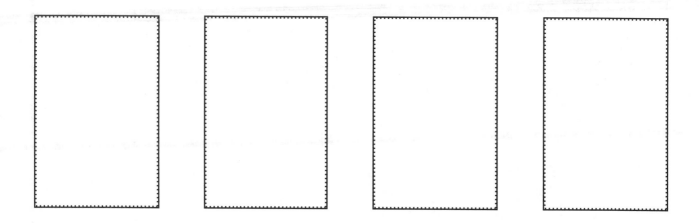

Pick 4 cards. Put them in order.
Record your work.

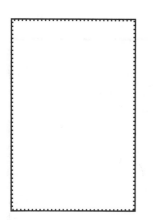   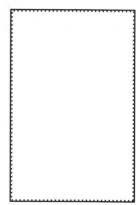

Snacks

Mia has 13 friends at her house for a party. She wants to give them each one snack. She has these snacks.

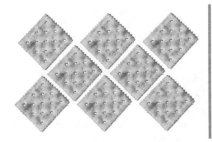  

Which snack does she have enough of for all of her friends and herself? Show how you know.

© Pearson Education K

What's the Same? 1

What's the same about the shapes in the circle? Draw arrows to show the other shapes that belong.

NOTE Students sort shapes based on a particular attribute.

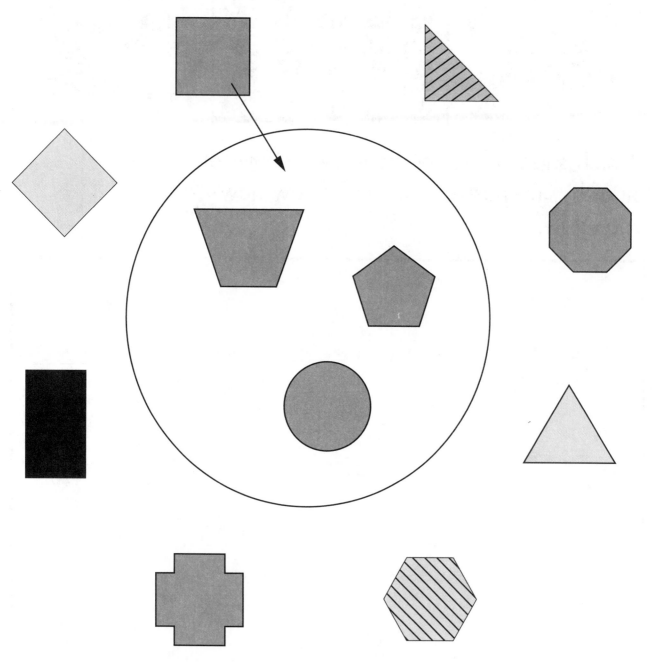

Patterns from Home

Dear Family,

   Our class is very excited about our work with patterns. Children are eager to display and share some of their work. We are currently setting up a special area in our classroom called "The Pattern Display" and are hoping that students will bring in patterns from home. Encourage your child to look for repeating patterns around your home. You might find repeating patterns in a piece of wallpaper, fabric, or flooring. There may be patterns on your dish towels, on a picture frame, or on a piece of clothing.

   Put your name on any item you send in. All items will be returned when our project is over. We will be careful with items from home. However, please do not send in anything that is breakable, valuable, or precious to you.

   You are welcome to come in to visit our Pattern Display. If you are interested, please let me know. We can arrange a time before, during, or after school.

   Thank you for your continued support of the work we are doing in our Kindergarten classroom.

What Comes Next?

Draw what comes next if the
pattern continues.

NOTE Students practice
extending repeating patterns.

□ ○ □ ○ □ ○ _____

🍎 🍊 🍌 🍎 🍊 🍌 _____

🔘 🌼 🔘 🌼 🔘 🌼 _____

Break the Train Recording Sheet

Color in your pattern. Show your cars.

How many cars? ____

Color in your pattern. Show your cars.

How many cars? ____

Color in your pattern. Show your cars.

How many cars? ____

Practice

What Comes Next?

Draw what comes next if the pattern continues.

NOTE Students practice extending repeating patterns.

_____

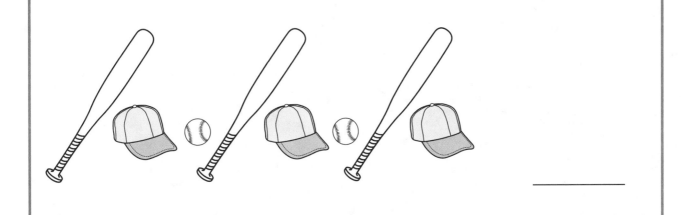

_____

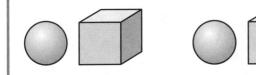 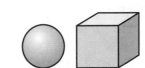

_____

12 Chips Recording Sheet

Color in your pattern.
Show your units.

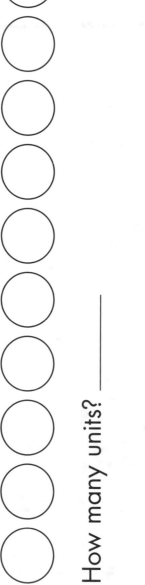

How many units? _____

How many units? _____

How many units? _____

A Pattern of Buttons

Jae decorated a picture frame with buttons. He made a pattern.

NOTE Students make a repeating pattern.

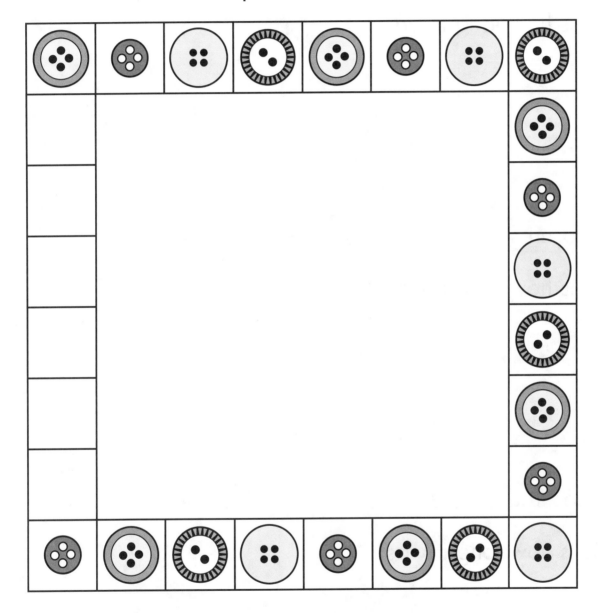

1. Some buttons are missing. Draw the missing buttons. Follow the pattern.

2. How many buttons are on the picture frame?

© Pearson Education K

Measuring Shoes

1. I measured _____'s shoe.

   This is how long it was:

2. I measured _____'s shoe.

   This is how long it was:

3. I measured _____'s shoe.

   This is how long it was:

Measuring with Sticks

We measured with this: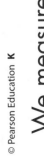

How long?

Letter

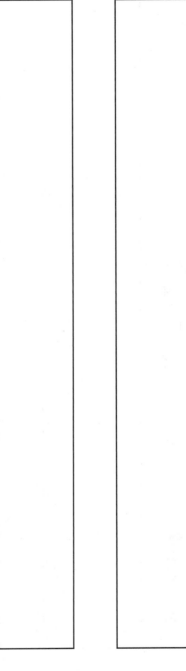

Measuring with Cubes

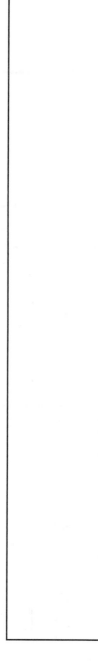

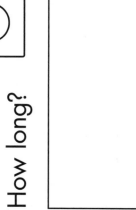

We measured with this:

How long?

Letter

Name _____   Date _____

Practice

How Many?

Record how many.

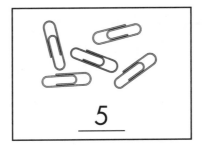

5

NOTE Students practice counting and writing numbers.

_____

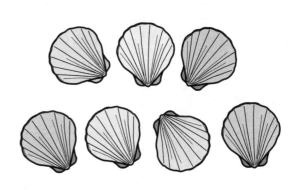

_____

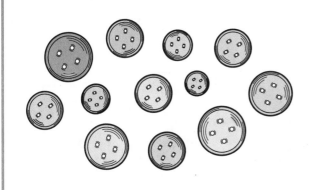

_____

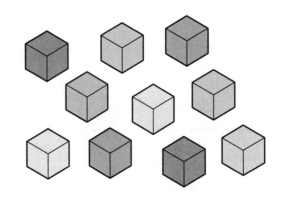

_____

Measuring and Counting

Ten-Frame

Grab and Count: Two Handfuls ✏️

Grab two handfuls. Show what you grabbed.
Show how many.

[ ]

Grab two handfuls. Show what you grabbed.
Show how many.

[ ]

Measuring Pictures

Record how many
cubes long each
object is.

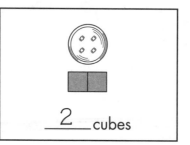

__2__ cubes

NOTE Students practice
counting and measuring
objects using cubes, a non-
standard measuring tool.

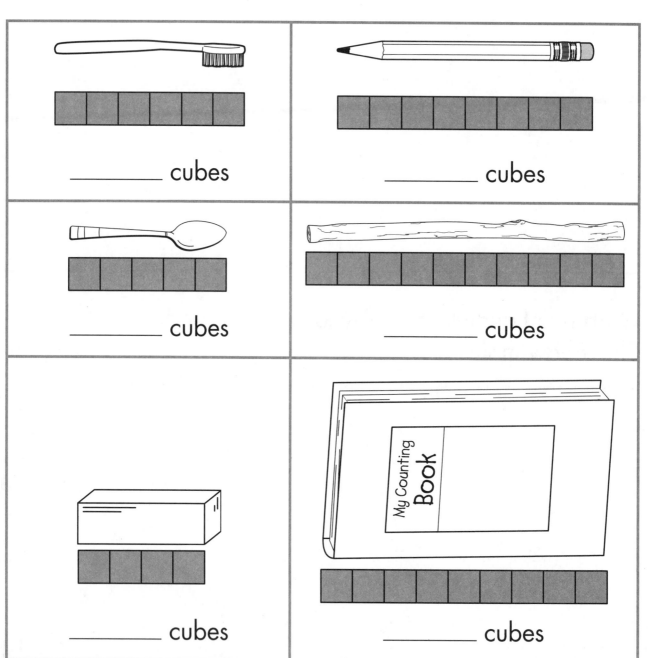

_____ cubes

_____ cubes

_____ cubes

_____ cubes

My Counting Book

_____ cubes

_____ cubes

Roll and Record 2 Recording Sheet

						9
						8
						7
						6
						5
						4
						3
						2

Racing Bears Gameboard

10	◯	◯	◯	◯
9				
8				
7				
6				
5				
4				
3				
2				
1				
0	☆ Start	☆ Start	☆ Start	☆ Start

One More, One Fewer

Starting Number	+1 or −1	Ending Total
	+1 −1	
	+1 −1	
	+1 −1	
	+1 −1	
	+1 −1	
	+1 −1	
	+1 −1	

Roll and Record
Write the total.

 + = __2__

NOTE Students combine two amounts to find the total.

 + = _____

 + = _____

 + = _____

 + = _____

Inch Grid Paper

Double Compare

  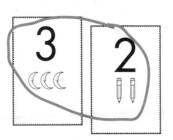

Circle the pair of cards in each row that shows more.

Toss the Chips

Game 1

Total Number: _____

Red ⬤	Yellow ◯

Game 2

Total Number: _____

Red ⬤	Yellow ◯

My Favorite Arrangement

NOTE Students count and solve a story problem.

Apples

Mia has 13 friends at her house. She wants to give each friend one apple. She has these apples.

1. How many apples does Mia have? _____

2. How many more apples does she need? Show your work.

Make a Shape, Build a Block   **Practice**

Color the Shapes

Color all of the squares ☐ blue.

Color all of the triangles ◺ red.

How many squares did you color? _____

How many triangles did you color? _____

Fill the Hexagons Gameboard

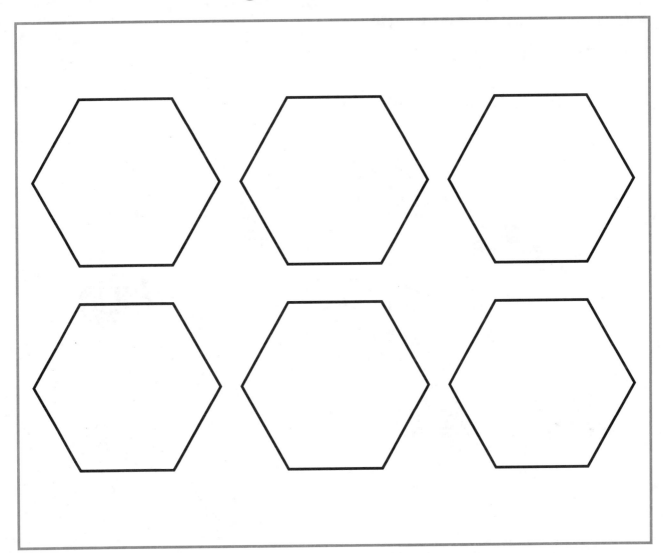

Sorting Buttons

What's the same about the
buttons in the circle?

Draw arrows to show the other
buttons that belong.

NOTE Students sort
buttons based on a
particular attribute.

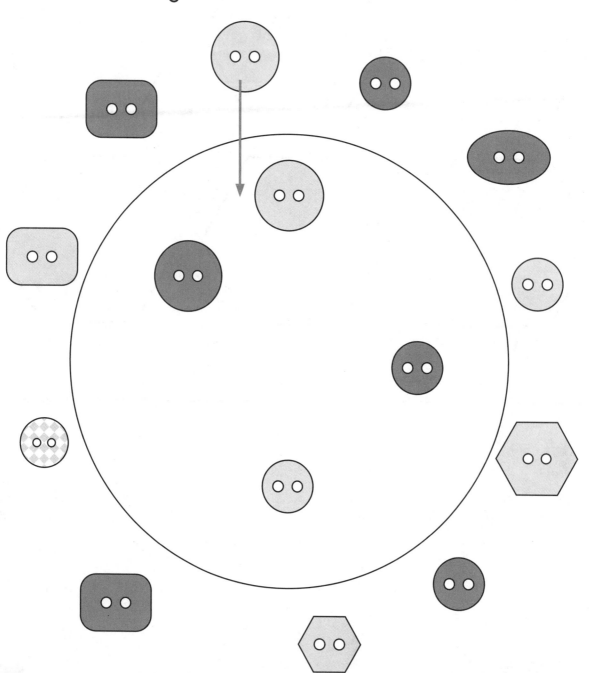

Make a Shape, Build a Block

Shape Hunt (page 1 of 2)

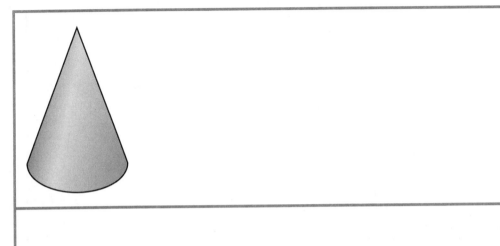

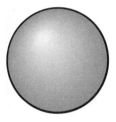

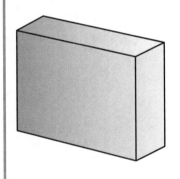

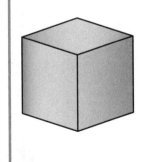

Make a Shape, Build a Block

Shape Hunt (page 2 of 2)

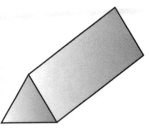

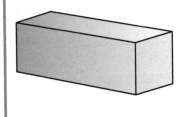

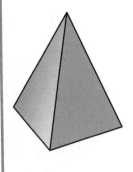

Shape Hunt at Home (page 1 of 2)

Dear Family,

   Your child will be going on a Shape Hunt at home to look for real-world objects that have these three-dimensional shapes. You can help by hunting for these shapes with your child and writing down all the different examples you find. You might help your child write the words or write them yourself as your child finds an object.

Sphere

Cylinder

Shape Hunt at Home (page 2 of 2)

Cube

Cone

Rectangular
prism

Matching Faces to Footprints

Match each Geoblock to a Geoblock footprint.

Geoblocks

Footprints

1.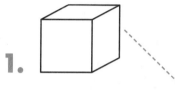

2.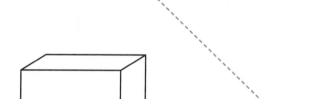

3.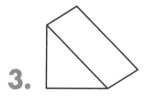

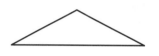

4.

5.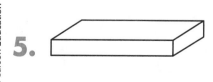

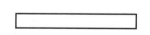

Can You Draw It?

NOTE Students draw shapes with specific attributes.

Draw these shapes. Use the dot paper to help you or to draw more shapes.

1. A shape with 3 sides

2. A shape with 4 sides

3. A shape with 6 sides

Make a Shape, Build a Block

Dot Paper

Inch Grid Paper

Toss the Chips

Game 1

Total Number: _____

Red ⬤	Yellow ◯

Game 2

Total Number: _____

Red ⬤	Yellow ◯

Racing Bears Gameboard

10	○	○	○	○
9				
8				
7				
6				
5				
4				
3				
2				
1				
0	☆ Start	☆ Start	☆ Start	☆ Start

Toss the Chips

Pretend you are playing *Toss the Chips* with 6 blue and white chips. Fill in the chart for the white chips.

NOTE Students practice counting and breaking a number into two parts (6 = 2 + 4).

Blue ●	White ○	Total Number 6
2		
1		
4		
3		
5		
6		

Name _____ Date _____

My Inventory Bag

Show what was in your bag.
Show how many.

Bag

Measuring Ourselves

Use cubes to measure parts of your body.
Record your measurements on the outline below.

Inventory Bags

Count the number of crayons, markers, and pencils.

Count how many there are in all.

NOTE Students practice counting and writing numbers.

_____ pencils

_____ crayons

_____ markers

How many are there in all? _____

Roll and Record 3 Recording Sheet

						10
						9
						8
						7
						6
						5
						4
						3
						2
						1
						0

More *Roll and Record*

Write the total.

NOTE Students combine two amounts to find the total.

•	+ •	= 2

(3 dots)	+ (5 dots)	= _____
(2 dots)	+ (1 dot)	= _____
(1 dot)	+ (3 dots)	= _____
(4 dots)	+ (2 dots)	= _____

Double Compare

Circle the pair of cards in each row that has more.

> **NOTE** Students combine two amounts and determine which total is greater.

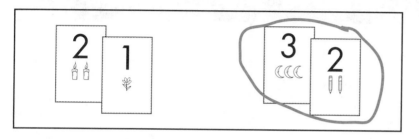

Build and Remove

Starting Number	Number to Remove	Ending Number
	−1 −2 −3	
	−1 −2 −3	
	−1 −2 −3	
	−1 −2 −3	
	−1 −2 −3	
	−1 −2 −3	

How Many Balls?

Read the problem. Show your work.

Emma was cleaning up after recess.

She found 3 balls by the swings.
She found 2 balls by the slide.

How many balls did Emma find?

How Many Grapes?

Read the problem. Show your work.

Mia brought grapes for snack.
She had 5 grapes.
Then she ate 1 of the grapes.

How many grapes did Mia have left?

How Many Blocks?

Read the problem. Show your work.

Jack was building with blocks.
He used 2 blocks to build a wall.
He used 4 blocks to build a bridge.

How many blocks did Jack use?

Five Crayons in All

Read the problem. Show your work.

I have 5 crayons in all.

Some are red and some are blue.
How many of each color could I have?

How many blues? How many reds?

Total of Six

In each row color the two cards that make 6.

NOTE Students practice counting and learning the combinations of two numbers that equal 6.

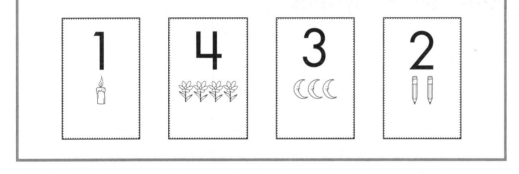

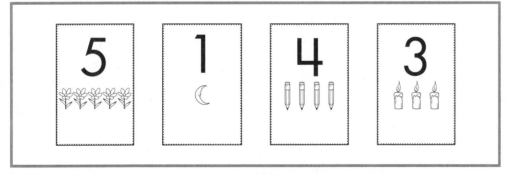

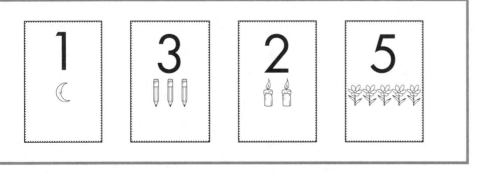

Six Crayons in All

Read the problem. Show your work.

I have 6 crayons in all.

Some are red and some are blue.
How many of each color could I have?

How many blues? How many reds?

Lots of Snacks

Kia has 3 kinds of crackers. If she has 9 crackers in all, how many of each kind can she have?

NOTE Students find combinations of numbers that make 9.

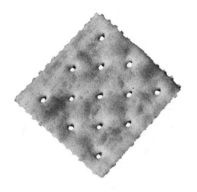  

™

Kia could have these crackers:

Kia could have these crackers:

™Courtesy Campbell Soup Company

Pattern Block Grab

Grab a handful of pattern blocks.
Show how many of each.

[ ]

How many did you grab in all? _____

Grab a handful of pattern blocks.
Show how many of each.

[ ]

How many did you grab in all? _____

Eyes at Home

Dear Family,

In class, we counted the number of eyes in our class. We will also be counting the number of eyes in students' homes.

Students will draw the eyes of each person at home on an index card. They should place the finished index cards into the envelope provided and write their name on the envelope.

If your child splits his or her time between different households, it's fine to include people from both homes.

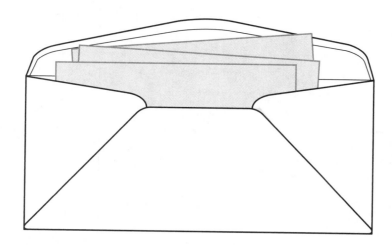

Counting Chairs

1. You can keep track of the number of chairs you count here.

2. How many chairs are in our class? _____

3. Are there enough chairs for everyone in

the class? _____

Eyes at Home

Choose an envelope. Count the number of people and the number of eyes. Record the data.

Name on Envelope	Number of People	Number of Eyes

How Many Eyes?
How Many Noses?

NOTE Students practice working with one-to-one and one-to-two relationships.

There are 4 people.

How many noses are there? _____

How many eyes   are there? _____

There are 7 people.

How many noses are there? _____

How many eyes   are there? _____

What's the Same? 2

What's the same about the flowers in the circle?

Color the other flowers that belong.

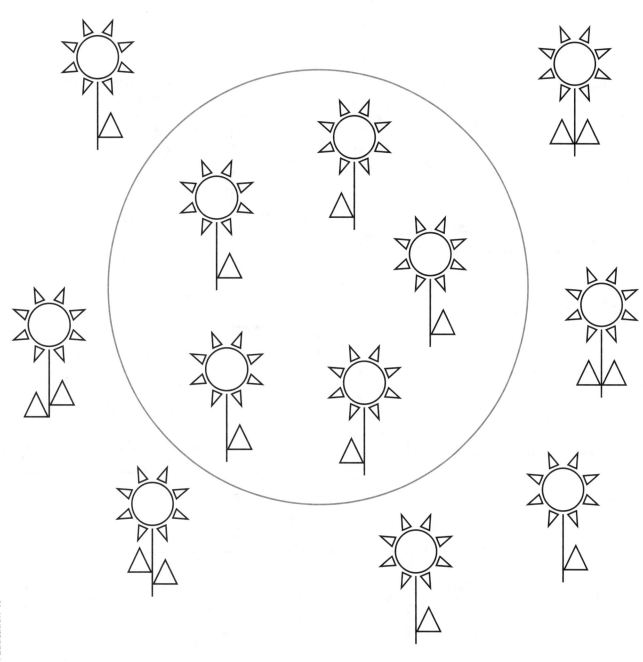

What's the Same? 3

Color the shapes that have 6 sides red.

Color the shapes that have 4 sides blue.

NOTE Students practice identifying and sorting shapes based on the number of sides.

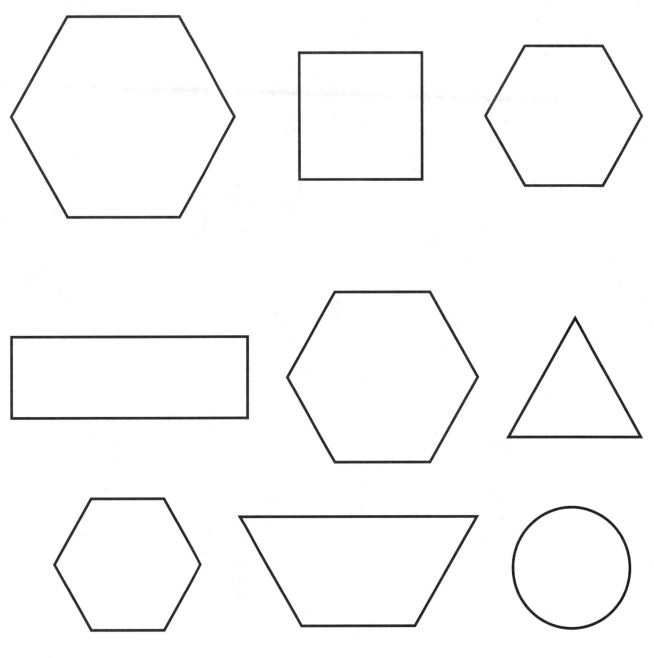

Name _____   Date _____

"Do You Like . . . ?" Survey Chart ✏️

Do you like _____?	
YES	**NO**

Favorite Meals

Beth asks her friends, "Which meal do you like best?" She marks their answers on the chart.

> **NOTE** Students analyze survey data and conduct a survey to collect data.

Breakfast	Lunch	Dinner
(4 figures)	(9 figures)	(6 figures)

1. How many people like breakfast best? _____

2. Which meal do most people like best? _____

3. How many people did Beth ask? _____

4. Ask some friends which meal they like best. Record your data. _____

Breakfast	Lunch	Dinner